Bringing your "one day" closer

Ricardo Collison

Published by:
The Parent Diary LLC
POX 843
Homewood 96141 CA, USA

ISBN: 978-1-7377348-4-0

Bringing your "one-day" closer

Overcome your limiting beliefs

Ricardo Collison

Forward:

With a dollop of sarcasm and bite-size, aha concepts, the author tells tales about his real-life transformational experiences. The stories are told to inspire, motivate, strip away limiting beliefs, and ask the uncomfortable questions that allow for growth.

This book is not just another inspirational self-help book. Instead, it's part of a series of books written to inspire all people who believe they are destined for more—written for those who have been held back by circumstance, environment, mindset, and more.

It's a collection of tales of the author's transformational journey from having nothing, being born a second-class citizen, to having everything his heart desired.

It's not a how-to guide to becoming an instant millionaire, although entirely possible with all the real-life tangible concepts. It is not a "do what I do, and you can be like me" guide.

We are all unique and have our own special gifts and greatness to bring to the world.

It's a series of books to help you change your mindset, help you think outside the box, and inspire a change in the narrative of your life, to live your best life.

Growing up and throughout our adult lives, we've realized how little information exists about how to change mindsets and how to change lives for people of color.

So we made it our mission to show that intentional thought can create and manifest the future you want, the future you choose.

At the Dream Cast Project, we want to inspire future generations to believe in the possible.

Dedicated to:

" All those communities of broken people, people who face such adversity yet still have hope for a better future for themselves and their families.

" To all people who are marginalized and experience discrimination and exclusion because of unequal power relationships across economic, political, social, and cultural dimensions.

" To all people who believe they are destined for more and who dared to dream bigger.

Chapters

CHAPTER 1

Bringing the "one day" closer

Have you ever used the words "one day" I will drive a car like that, own my house, start a business, be happy, and find a loving partner? Or one day I will have enough money to travel the world?

What are you waiting for? Why not bring your one-day closer today?

This morning, Wednesday 10th August 2022. I woke up at 5:18 am with a crazy idea. An idea I could only dare share with my wife, Michele, at 6:30 am. You see, sleep is very important to her. So unless the house is burning, I would not dare wake her up.

At 6:31 am, I gently shook her by her shoulder and said, "I have something exciting to tell you."

Her response was, "have you made coffee yet?"

"No," I said, "but I had this crazy idea to help inspire people to bring their one-day closer. I want to write an inspirational mini-ebook to inspire others to think outside the box.

And I want to attempt writing this book within ten days, release it to the world for free, and prove that you can bring the One-Day closer, even in just ten days. What do you think? It's a tight deadline, but not impossible."

Her response was short and sweet, "that's awesome; you better get started; wake me up when coffee is ready."

So I started on the coffee and writing this book.

I have to admit it's not just about meeting a deadline to show that you can bring your one-day closer or penning a free mini ebook bestseller.

I've met countless deadlines in my corporate career and personal life. I've just made some of these deadlines by the hair on my chinny chin, and I'm sure many of you have had similar experiences.

You know the ones I mean, deadline experiences that fall just short of miracle status. Penning this book in 10 days will surely fall into the "it's a miracle I made it" status.

So, if the book you're reading is first published before the 21st of August 2022, you have witnessed a miracle.

For me, it's not about the deadline; that shit is easy to beat. You don't have to be a Jack Bower to meet a deadline, even in an end-of-world deadline scenario.

Writing this mini-book, in my self-set tight deadline, is about overcoming my personal "one day" of writing and publishing a book, even if it's just a short format book. It's about conquering my limiting beliefs about not being good enough to become a writer or believing that my command of the English language is poor or mediocre at best.

It's about overcoming the limiting belief that I am not good enough to produce written content for mass consumption or anything more than my small Facebook following.

These limiting beliefs were reinforced over years of me barely passing English at school.

And years of having my spelling errors publicly pointed out on social media posts (a Dick and Karen move, by the way).

The lack of confidence in my English writing ability led me to rely on team members, who reported to me, to double-check my spelling and grammar before I sent an important email.

I bet there is bound to be someone reading this saying, "ahh, another poor me story."

No, this could not be further from the truth. I speak four languages and have lived in five countries.

I get to swim in the Mediterranean every day in summer and ski out of our backyard in winter. This is anything but a poor me story. It's a story of how our family has and how you can overcome the limiting beliefs that hold you back from your "one-day" dreams.

I'll share a formula that, if applied, will have you happy and winning for the rest of your life.

You may wonder why I would like to share this formula with you. It's because one day, I believe you will be brave enough to share your story with the world and inspire others.

I hope that your "one-day" story will someday inspire someone else to their greatness. I believe this is how we change the world for the better through sharing without expecting anything back.

CHAPTER 2

Born a product of humanity's shittyness, full of limiting beliefs.

Limiting belief is a topic I sometimes wish I were not so qualified to speak or write about. That said, my history cannot be changed; it's who I am. It forged me through the good and the bad.

I was born, a product of the apartheid government in South Africa, to a teenage mother, a jailbird biological father, and an abusive stepdad. No one I knew had completed high school or attended college.

My early childhood was spent living in a two-bedroom government assistance apartment with nine other people. Yes, you read that correctly. My grandparents, their six kids, and I lived in one two-bedroom flat.

I spent all of my childhood in a society where people who looked like me, were classified as people of a lesser race. Because of the color of our skin, we were deemed less intelligent, less beautiful, and less worthy.

I grew up in Parkwood, Cape Town, in a deprived socio-economic area with known rapists, robbers, murders, and abusers living within the community. In this community of broken people, I knew many who would face such daily adversity yet still had hope and strived for a better future for themselves and their families. This community managed to produce me and continues to create many others like me.

I'm that same little boy that grew up in the chaos of destitution and poverty—this mess of hate, love, and hope. But, I can talk about crazy dreams becoming a reality because most of mine have come true. No fairy dust made them happen, no winning lotto ticket, no rich uncle, just my belief in being more than others thought I could be.

Removing or reprogramming my limiting beliefs, I believe, was one of the reasons I was able to achieve my "one day."

If you want to get to your "one day" dream, you, too, will need to reprogram your limiting beliefs.

Combining this with perseverance, a change in mindset, and taking action will make you feel like you have a magic wand you can wield to create any reality you choose.

My wife and I now live a nomadic / world schooler life with our amazing kiddos. Since our exit from corporate life, we have started five businesses and now run Dream Cast Project, an organization established to show kids and young adults their dreams are possible, irrespective of their background.

And that letting go of limiting beliefs and taking the necessary action will bring that one-day dream closer.

I'm sharing some of my life experiences in this book, not to be a boastful a-hole. But as a token of validity for the rest of this book. None of the content you are reading is fabricated. I share these genuine life experiences as examples of what is possible and to inspire. Your future success will ultimately make the world a better place for everyone. So jump into it.

CHAPTER 3

What are limiting beliefs, and where do they come from?

> " "No one wants to hear about what they could have been, even if it's from themselves"
> - Ricardo Collison.

- I have to work hard to earn money.
- I'm not smart enough.
- I'm not worthy.
- I'm too old or too young.
- I don't have enough experience.
- I need lots of money to start a business.
- Girls don't play soccer or become astronauts.
- Money is the root of all evil.
- Money does not grow on trees - maybe this one is true.

Do any of these sound familiar? You may have heard these limiting beliefs or something similar from your parents or friends at some point in your life. But, unfortunately, if you accept it as a truism, you have robbed yourself of your true potential.

At this point that most people stop reading because self-reflection is hard. No one wants to hear about what they could have been, even if it's from themselves.

Limiting beliefs are nothing more than other people's perceptions that you have been told, sometimes by people closest to you. I equate limiting beliefs to the construct of the religious beliefs you were born with.

You did not ask to be born into a specific religion and socialized with its practices and beliefs, but you were. Practices and beliefs you may question later in life and formulate your own opinion. You can do the same with the limiting beliefs holding you back.

Your limiting beliefs are conscious and subconscious thoughts creeping into your daily life and telling you something that is ultimately NOT true.

It does not matter what religion, race, or socio-economic circumstances you were born into. You have been fortunate enough to experience life. This means you have the same amount of time in a day as any other person on this earth, irrespective of race, color, or status.

How you choose to spend that time is entirely up to you.

Your time is the gift that life has generously given you. Your 1-400 trillion chance of life also comes with your freedom of thought, and your thoughts and actions are what create your reality. Your thought and the corresponding action will bring you closer to your "one day".

CHAPTER 4

Our life experience puts us in a box.

"Show me your friends, and I'll show you your future" — **Dan Pena.**

Limiting beliefs are assumptions about your reality that come from your life experiences, like what you're told, where you were born, your socio-economic circumstances, etc.

I grew up in an impoverished Cape-coloured community, and a phrase still rings in my head from time to time is "Jy hoe jou wit." This Afrikaans phrase means, "you behave like a white person of privilege." It was because I dared to dream big about traveling, sports cars, and living in a beautiful home. However, dreaming big was not the norm where I grew up. Success and big dreams were the reality reserved for white people, which I was not.

Years later, this ridicule persisted by the same childhood acquaintances.

However, this time it was because my accent had changed due to living abroad in the UK, Switzerland, USA, and Spain for the last 20+ years.

How ironic, even though I had traveled the world in these 20+ years, this ridicule persisted. I was still being ridiculed years later for stepping outside the lines the society I grew up in painted for me, the box they put me in.

CHAPTER 5

Overcoming any limiting beliefs you may have?

So, how did I overcome my limiting beliefs? And how do you?

First, be kind to yourself and know that you are a product of your socio-economic environment, friends, family, education, and religion. Also, know that this environment is constantly evolving as you go through life and that you start having more control over it as you get older.

The second is to understand your limiting beliefs and in which area of your life they may exist.

There are four general categories.

1. Limiting beliefs about money and abundance

2. Limiting beliefs about relationships

3. Limiting beliefs about your abilities

4. Limiting beliefs about health and wellbeing

I will use money and abundance as an example, as it has been the closest limiting belief I have needed to overcome for a long time.

For most of my childhood, I had aunts and uncles say that money is the root of all evil. The environment I grew up in made this a truism, unfortunately. The mindset in the community was that if you had lots of money, you either stole it or sold drugs for it.

Both were bound to get you into trouble, hence the mindset that money is the root of all evil.

For years I lived with this belief and the belief that "money is the root of all evil" and "you have to work hard for your money."

I naturally unknowingly carried these beliefs into early adulthood. My limiting beliefs were validated by everyone around me, my mother, stepfather, uncles, and aunts. They all spoke about how hard they worked for their money, how stressful it was and that there was never enough. Does any of this sound familiar to you?

❝ "Your beliefs become your thoughts, Your thoughts become your words, Your words become your actions, Your actions become your habits, Your habits become your values, Your values become your destiny." — Gandhi

Today my wife and I work 2-4 hours a day doing what we love, a far cry from the beliefs we were fed when we were younger. It's taken a long time to re-program those limiting beliefs, but it is possible.

Had we not started reprogramming our thinking, we would no doubt still be working 9-12 hours a day, if not longer.

You see, money is NOT the root of all evil. Greed and selfishness are the root of all evil.

You don't have to work hard for your money, just smarter.

You DO deserve to be wealthy.

You DESERVE abundance in all areas of your life.

Why? Because you were not born to be a slave, to be unhappy or unfulfilled. No, you got this chance in life to be everything you can be.

CHAPTER 6

Identifying your limiting beliefs and changing them

Your beliefs and habits are some of the hardest things to change in your life. It's not easy and will take continuous work. If you've ever been a smoker, you will know how hard it is to quit.

Changing your habits and reprogramming your limiting beliefs is an iterative process.

Your limiting beliefs will not suddenly go away; you must constantly work on changing them. I found that what works best for me is to create affirmations from each reframed belief that I want to change.

I've used the following few steps to change and reprogram my limiting beliefs.

- Identify what limiting beliefs you may have.
- Recognize that it is just a belief.
- Challenge your own beliefs.
- Realize that your limiting beliefs are potentially damaging.
- Reframe your limiting belief "it's possible" beliefs.
- Take action on new beliefs.

Example:

- **Limiting belief** - Money is the root of all evil.

- **Recognize** - I recognize that this belief comes from someone that may have said this to you at some point

- **Challenge:** Many people with money make the world a better place.

- **Realize:** If I believe money is the route to all evil, it may damage my potential to use money as a tool to do good in the world.

- **Reframe:** Money is just a tool I can use to do good and make the world a better place for myself and my family.

- **Take action:** Revisit your reframed "it's possible" beliefs often, write them down, and use them as affirmations.

Sometimes it's not easy to identify limiting beliefs so I've listed a common few I've come across. I have also reframed them as examples of the above process.

Hopefully, it will make it easier for you to identify the ones holding you back and help you reframe them positively.

Limiting beliefs about money and abundance (and how to reframe them as positive affirmations)

- Earning money requires working really hard *vs. I put my money to work for me.*

- I never win free things *vs. I have enough money to buy what I need.*

- I will never get my big break *vs. I have been so fortunate so far and will continue to be*

- There is never enough *vs. money is abundant, and there is enough for everyone.*

- Everyone else gets all the good stuff *vs. I am blessed with so much and continue to be.*

- I have to protect what I've got because there just isn't enough *vs. The world is abundant; there is more than enough for everyone.*

- You just can't trust others with money *vs. I trust the people I surround myself with.*

- Taxes are evil *vs. Taxes are needed to build a better society, I am happy to pay my fair share.*

- I just don't know how to manage money *vs. Every day; I am learning to manage my money better.*

- I will never be rich *vs. I have the potential to be anything I put my mind to.*

- You can't trust someone who has a lot of money *vs. People are generally good; money is just a tool that can be used to do good or bad,*

- If I had a better education, I could earn more money *vs. I have the potential to be anything I put my mind to.*

Limiting beliefs about relationships

- I will never find love vs. I'm happy with who I am and open to a loving relationship.

- I am not worthy of being loved vs. I am worthy of love and much more.

- My relationships just never work out vs. I am a compassionate and loving person.

- Putting yourself out there only results in getting hurt vs. I attract good loving people

- I am not good enough on my own vs. I am worthy and good enough.

- My family is always trying to keep me down vs. I am in control of my own destiny, my "one day" dreams.

- Love never works out for me vs. I have so much to offer the partner I choose

Limiting beliefs about work

- It's impossible to make money doing what you love *vs. I am always working on making money doing what I love*

- I am not talented *vs. I have unique gifts and talents that are needed and valuable.*

- I have no unique strengths *vs. I am discovering my unique strengths every day*

- I am not good enough *vs. I am good enough.*

- I just don't have enough experience *vs. I can learn anything I put my mind to.*

- I just don't know how to manage big projects *vs. I am competent and getting better everyday.*

- My opinion isn't important *vs. My opinion is important and valuable.*

Limiting beliefs about self-worth

- I am a failure *vs. I am on track to my own greatness*

- I can't make things happen *vs. Good things are happening for me everyday*

- I don't deserve a better life *vs. I deserve to live my best life.*

- It's all my parents' fault *vs. My future is dependent on my own actions*

- That's just my luck! *vs. Opportunities are always proceeding themselves to me*

- Who am I to have everything I have ever wanted? *vs. I was born to share my gifts with the world and live my best life*

Limiting beliefs about good health

-

- My body just heals slowly *vs. I am doing everything to help my body heal*

- Getting sick is unavoidable *vs. I am healthy and look after my body*

- I don't deserve to be healthy *vs. My health enables me to help others*

- Everyone else in my family is overweight *vs. I work diligently to control my weight*

- I am helpless to heal myself *vs. I am taking every action to heal my body and mind*

CHAPTER 7

Kick negative thoughts in the nuts and bring your one-day closer.

Another thing I do when facing negative thoughts, limiting beliefs, or comments that contradict my goals is to dismiss them entirely. Do not spend any time thinking about them or whether or not they are possible. Do not try to disprove them or put them into a decisional matrix. Doing this is not worth your time, it will send you down a rabbit hole from which you will never emerge with anything valuable. Just completely dismiss them.

Personally, when a negative thought enters my mind. I shout at it like a rabid dog, "Get Out, Get OUT, GET OUT OF MY HEAD!".

Once I've regained control of my thoughts. I replace all negative thoughts with positive thoughts and repeat this mantra to myself, "Every day, in every way, everything is getting better and better ."

I really do this; it's my thing, my mantra if you like. Feel free to borrow mine or come up with your own. It works to displace shitty thoughts.

I'm suggesting this because when you start thinking about why you can't succeed, you place your mind in a negative state. When your mind is in this state, very little is possible.

Your negative thoughts will immobilize you.

You will come up with more reasons why you cannot do it, than why you can. Sound familiar; I bet it does! Negative thoughts attract negative outcomes, and positive thoughts attract positive outcomes.

CHAPTER 8

The one-day, mayday, mayday.

One day I found myself fortunate enough to fly in a small airplane with a friend.

My friend, who was keen to influence me to become a pilot, was also the owner of the small airplane.

I had always wanted to be a sports pilot and read and studied voraciously about the topic before I ever got inside a cockpit. But, as the universe would have it, my friend let me take the controls that day once we hit cruising altitude.

I'm flying an airplane; I'm flying a fucking airplane to Las Vegas. I can hardly believe it; holy shit, I'm experiencing one of my one-days.

As we climb past 10.000ft in altitude in the Cessna Skyhawk, we are required to supplement the oxygen that we breathe through a little tube contraption we place by our nose. This tube releases pure O2. It is simple enough and does not interfere with the headphones you're wearing or constrict any of your movements.

My friend ensures that my breathing tube is placed correctly on my nose, and then the unthinkable happens—my friend slumps over in his seat. The lack of oxygen at a high altitude has caused him to black out. My "one day" has just arrived, and I'm not ready for it - shit.

Shit, the fuckening is happening,

"The fuckening definition" - When your day is going suspiciously well, and you don't trust it, then something shit finally goes down. "Ah-ha, there it is, the fuckening"

At this point, a few things happen to me simultaneously. First, a massively elevated heart rate, sweating profusely from everywhere, disbelieve that this fuckening is actually happening, and then reality sets in.

How much do I want to live vs. the possibility of dying today, dying in about 2-3 hours, to be exact? That's how much flying time we have left and how much time I have to solve this problem.

In moments like these, you need to give your self-belief a double dose of BIY12 (belief in yourself x 12). You have to call on that Champion inside of you. You have to push all your limiting beliefs to the deep dark far end in your mind, so far back that it falls out of your butthole and vanishes down the toilet.

Needless to say, I was not ready to die that day. I took control of the airplane, descended as smoothly as possible to about 5000ft, opened the little side flap window to let more air into the cabin, and kept following the GPS instrumentation on the dashboard. A few minutes later, my friend regained consciousness and was very grateful that I was able to take control and apologized emphatically for the incident. To this day, I still don't know if my friend faked this incident or if it was just a misstep in safety protocol.

Nonetheless, I'm sharing this life event because I was able to take some great lessons from it.

1. Even when you think things are impossible, you can always find a way to change the circumstance you are in - if you really want to and take the needed action. Even when you are woefully unqualified to fly an airplane as I was.

2. You will never be 100% ready for anything you attempt in your life. It does not matter if you don't have the qualification, experience, or knowledge. These are all things that you pick up quickly along the way.

3. We all have some form of the above experience in our lives. Even though this was an extreme life and death example of letting go of limiting beliefs. It is not so different from what you and I experience daily to overcome our limiting beliefs. Think of it this way. You have already removed some of your limiting beliefs by applying for or starting a new job. When you ask someone on a date or enter a new relationship. Even something like learning to ride a bike for the first time. Initially, you believed that you couldn't ride a bike; you fell a few times, got back in the saddle, fell a few more times, and got back in the saddle. And then suddenly, it clicked, you did

not fall, you are riding a bike, the wind is blowing in your hair, and you are in complete control of where you point the front wheel. It's a simple example of overcoming limiting beliefs, but we always seem to take it for granted once we have accomplished our goal.

4. Leveraging our previous successes is the quickest way to reprogram your limiting beliefs. Your previous successes should be the fuel that helps you overcome your next challenge. For example, suppose you've succeeded in getting one of the many jobs you applied for. In that case, the probability of repeating the process becomes easier. If you started one business, your next business would be easier to start, etc.

Changing limiting beliefs is a hard thing to do, but not impossible. With continued practice, it becomes a subconscious program that just runs in the back of your head. I call this program "the janitor." It's one of the most important programs you can install into your subconscious mind. This program will bring all of your one-days closer by removing any limiting beliefs you may have.

CHAPTER 9

Your Champion and the bully

At this point, I want to introduce you to your Champion. Yes, your Champion, we all have one, and yours is incredible. Your Champion comprises the bravest, wisest, most innovative, kindest, most self-confident, and empathetic parts of you.

It's the superhero part of you who you may already have been introduced to. The one who jumped out to save the day when there was a problem to solve at work. The one who came out when you needed to help a friend through a difficult time. The one who baked the most amazing cupcakes, which everyone complimented you on. It's that you when you feel your best, and when you feel your best, you can do amazing things.

Now we would all like to feel on top of the world all the time.

But unfortunately, we have another non-superhero lurching in the shadows called Mr. Negative Self-Talk, Mr. Shit for short.

Your Champion and Mr. Shit live in the same place, your head. Mr. Shit is always trying to influence your Champion. For example, when your Champion sees an opportunity to do something amazing, like start a new job or business, travel, or move to a different country.

Mr. Shit is saying to your Champion, "but what if you fail, what if you are wrong, it's too dangerous, you won't make it, it's too difficult, stay here by me where it's uncomfortable but safe".

Many times we talk ourselves down from reaching for our dreams. It's a combination of Mr negative self-talk and fear. So let's concentrate on getting rid of Mr negative self-talk and letting your Champion out more. Once this becomes second nature, your Champion can then tackle fear head-on.

CHAPTER 10

Give your "one-day" dream a chance.

What will it take for you to give your dream a chance? Your "one-day" I'll start my own business, leave a toxic relationship, travel to the place you have always wanted to go, etc.,

What will it take to say yes to your greatness for more than just 24 hours?

Yes? We see this all the time - people get inspired by some inspirational content they watch or read. Or they may be fortunate enough to be inspired by a friend who has opted to let their Champion out more.

And then, after 24 hours, nada, nothing, zilch changes. They pack their 'one-day' back into their 'some-day' suitcase.

Your Champion has been defeated without even trying or giving her/him a chance. Mr negative self-talk is content and smug in his uncomfortable little world. Knowing that he managed to defeat the greatness you have within you without even stepping into the ring of life. Sad, but true.

Michele and I gave our "one-day" dream a chance when we were finally brave enough to step outside the box we'd been painted in. Brave enough to overcome our limiting beliefs and fears and take the leap of faith to move across the globe to London, UK.

It's no secret that we were scared shitless the first time we took this leap of faith to reach for our "one day". The "one day" of living in London, making lots of money, and perfecting our pommy accent.

Stepping outside of the box is scary. This is normal; it is supposed to be scary. It's the type of scary caution that has kept us alive for thousands of years as primitive men and women.

However, once you step outside the box, you start developing a completely different mindset, one of possibility. And you will find that the next time you step outside the box and take a risk, it will be a bit easier and a little less scary.

How do I know?

The first time we moved countries, we lost everything we had within two months. By month two of living in London, we had less than 300 GBP in our bank account to make it through the month. We could not even afford to pay our rent for the following month.

However, it's amazing how innovation and self-preservation skills kick in when you are under pressure. For example, to pay for the next month's rent, I offered to build our landlord a website for his business. If I could not do this by the date the rent was due, I would have to give him my laptop as payment. Michele, on the other hand, took a job at a waste disposal company. She had to travel to the outskirts of London every day. Still, we survived and had just enough money to buy food and cover travel expenses.

We figured that if this experience did not kill us, what was stopping us from pushing ahead and applying for positions we may have been underqualified for on paper?

Within the next 12 months, we were both permanently employed. We rented a large 4-story home and sublet the rooms for additional income.

We managed to secure a working visa to stay in the country and saved up enough money to buy our first apartment in London.

Making this "one-day" dream of moving to another country a reality, was a scary and extremely humbling experience.

However, this experience made the next four country moves easier.

Had we not given our one-day dream and chance, who knows where we would be today?

I can confidently say that we would not have had all our fantastic experiences. We'd not have met our amazing friends or traveled the world multiple times. We would not have had all the opportunities that presented themselves to us. We were no longer in a box, and the opportunities were endless.

Suppose you never take the chance on your "one day", never use your previous wins as mental fuel, and never take action.

I don't know what the exact outcome will be but I do know that the probability of reaching your dream or potential would be highly diminished. The world is full of opportunities; you just need to be willing to see them.

CHAPTER 11

What's holding you back from your "one day"?

" "Don't wait; the time will never be just right."
- Napoleon Hill.

You are alive and healthy. A free and thinking human being. You are not chained to a pole like a bad guard dog or marooned on an island hoping for a passing ship to save you.

There is for all intents and purposes only one thing holding you back from your "one day", YOU!

Your state of mind and limiting beliefs keep you from achieving everything you desire. This may sound counterintuitive even if you have heard this before but bear with me and let me explain.

We tend to focus on what we feel is working against us. We, more often than not, listen to Mr. Negative self-talk instead of focusing on the positive and letting our champion out.

We do this subconsciously because that is where our limiting beliefs reside. It's the same place that Mr. Negative self-talk and your champion live. In your head, and the wonderful thing about this truism is that it's your head, and you can consciously control what goes on inside of it.

What we need to do instead is consciously focus on everything we have going for us or regularly recall our previous accomplishments. The latter will do wonders for your confidence and self-esteem.

Many times people use their circumstances as an excuse for not being able to achieve their desires. Excuses like, I don't have the education to get that job, I don't have the money to make my idea a reality, I'm too fat, dark, tall, short, round, it's not the right time, and the list goes on and on. Does any of these sound familiar? This is a list of excuses fueled by limiting beliefs.

No one with a negative mindset has ever thought their way to a million dollars, a loving relationship, or a profitable business; it's just not possible. This is like saying, "I want to date Charlize Theron, but I am too fat, too short, too skinny, too round; she will never want to date me." With this type of thinking, you have just shot and sent your dreams and desires to where all dead dreams and goals go - the one-day dream graveyard.

So instead, start focusing on the positive; what have you got going for you right now?

For a start, you took your first breath of this new day, and you've taken the first step to changing your reality by reading or listening to this book.

Start by writing down all the positive things you have going in your life, from the smallest to the biggest. Then, put yourself in the shoes of someone who has lost everything: their job, house, health.

You will quickly see how many positive things you have going for you.

CHAPTER 12

Your What if's redefined

Because of our higher level of cognitive ability as humans, and our ability to think, we are always playing out what-if scenarios in our heads. But unfortunately, we still have a lot of the ape-man fight or flight DNA ruling our actions. Therefore our default "what if's" are almost always negative.

It sounds like this, what if we leave the cave and something eats us? What if the business fails, people do not like me, and what if the airplane crashes?

We run through all these negative "what ifs" even before we start. And then, we never start.

But there is also another way of thinking.

What if you succeeded? What if your business was highly successful? What if you found the love of your life?

What if the people you met while traveling exceeded your expectations? What if you could not fail? The latter is a big one.

What would you attempt to do if you could not fail? How full out would you play, and how much would you use your imagination to create the world you want?

How much would you care what other people thought?

One of my "what if's" happened in 2008. I had started a new job in London, which did not work out quite as planned, and I was subsequently fired - not the best thing to help build your self-esteem, but it happens to the best of us. Not only was I fired, but the company I was working for had applied for my working visa which gave us the ability to live and work in the United Kingdom.

No longer being employed by them meant that in the next 28 days, I'd be in the country illegally. If I did not find another company to hire me and apply for my work permit I would have to pack my bags and head back to South Africa or risk being deported. The latter was a thought that crossed my mind more than a few times.

I jumped into action and I applied for every position my skill base allowed me to. Michele pitched in and started submitting my resume to companies for jobs we both knew I was missing the required qualifications and experience for.

I said to Michele, "what are you doing? I don't have the necessary qualifications; I'll never get the interview; it's a waste of time." She responded, "What if you are exactly what they are looking for?"

A few days later, I received an invitation to interview with Mediacom, eBay, and Amazon. A few weeks later, after the interviews, I received an offer of employment from all three companies.

If we did not redefine our "what if's", we would not have found ourselves living in Switzerland only a few weeks later.

It's amazing what a shift in thought will do for you. Will you always win? No, but your chances of succeeding are exponentially better. So what if you failed a few times but got up every time and then succeeded?

So shift your mindset from a "what if" negative to a "what if" positive.

CHAPTER 13

How would the world be a better place if your "one day" became a reality?

I always think of this in the context of my previous employment. My teams and I made the companies we worked for a lot of money, hundreds of millions of dollars. Yet, nothing I did made the world a better place. It enabled me to put food on the table and a roof over my family's head. It allowed me to take a 2-week vacation every year, which honestly was not a vacation. It was more like just working somewhere else but the office. I'm sure you've experienced something similar.

At some point in our lives, we are just cogs in a machine. Cogs in the global economic machine controlled by a few. Imagine if we were the cogs in our own machine making this world what we wanted it to be. Imagine how your "one-day" dream could make a difference in the world.

There are quite a few examples of how people have reached their "one-day" dream and made the world a better place.

Toms Shoes - founder Blake Mycoskie. The idea came from a trip to Argentina in 2006, where Blake saw the hardships faced by children without shoes, from a lack of basic protection to the inability to attend school. For every pair of TOMS shoes purchased, a pair of new shoes is given to a child in need in partnership with humanitarian organizations. Dream Cast Project has followed in the footsteps of the pioneer by providing one journal to an underprivileged child for every one purchased.

Sexy Socks - Founder, Dave Hutchison, discovered the harsh reality that many South African children go to school without a pair of socks to wear. A socially-driven company was born determined to make a difference. The company not only donates a pair of school socks for every pair of Sexy Socks sold but also does what they call sock drops. An initiative where they visit schools to deliver socks and talk to the students about social entrepreneurship and the upliftment of communities.

WakaWaka - Founder, Maurits Groen. The story began in 2010, with the World Cup in South Africa. He found that millions of people didn't have access to electricity in the country. A seed was planted... something needed to change and WakaWaka was born. The name comes from Shakira's opening song of the 2010 World Cup and it's the Swahili translation for 'shine bright'. Since then, donated WakaWaka solar lamps have helped 50,000 Haitians following that country's 2010 earthquake, over 100,000 survivors of typhoon Haiyan in the Philippines, over 60,000 people fighting Ebola in Liberia and Sierra Leone, and well over 400,000 Syrian refugees.

But we don't all have the set of skills required to enter politics or to become a CEO of a company. So the question remains: can we still make the world better with our "one day"?

The answer is yes; even though you don't have the power to single-handedly abolish racism, solve income inequality or clean the great Pacific garbage patch, you do have the power to inspire others.

You have the power to inspire others to reach for their "one day" by leading by example. Helping others believe they can do the same is the key to making the world a better place.

Whether your "one day" is to start a community counseling organization as Tanya Jenniker did with Deep Healing Counseling. Or start an accounting service business like Lynn Connolly, who started "In the Black" because of her "one-day" passion for helping small to medium-sized companies with their accounting needs.

Your "one day" is needed not only to inspire others to their "one day," but in the process, you may be creating thousands of jobs, enriching the lives of thousands of others, creating a product that helps our world heal, or just living your best, most fulfilled life.

When we think about starting a new business or partnering with someone, this is the first thing we ask ourselves: how will it make the world a better place? Of course, there are many ways to make money. Still, you will always find the ones that are the most intrinsically rewarding are the ones that are in service of others. This is one of the reasons why the Dream Cast Project exists, to show kids and young adults that their dreams are possible

CHAPTER 14

There is a lot of space on top

Here is a fun fact for you: In the first quarter of 2022, 69.1 percent of the total wealth in the United States was owned by the top 10 percent of earners. In comparison, the lowest 50 percent of earners only owned 2.8 percent of the total wealth. - statista.com

A misconception and limiting belief is holding back many people from their "one day." It is the misconception that it's hard to get to the top, that there is very little space on top. This could not be further from the truth.

Ask yourself, how many business owners do you know vs. how many people do you know who work for business owners? Yes, it's a staggering inverse of this misconception that we have. There is a lot more space at the top than you think.

The truth is that we cannot all be at the top, but we can strive for a more equal distribution of wealth. Unfortunately, the current economic system is designed to ensure there is a workforce to keep the cogs of the machine going. Many factors make up this design that is outside of our control. Factors like socio-economic circumstance, education, and dare I say, the color of your skin - how crazy is that last one? However, even though there may be factors outside of your control that contribute to your own economic improvement. There is one factor that weighs more than any other.

It's not who you know, where in the social hierarchy you were born, your skin color, lack of equal opportunity, or even your current knowledge. Instead, the thing that weighs most against you is YOU!

Yes, you. Your mindset, belief, and willingness to take the road less traveled are holding you back. Nothing ventured, nothing gained.

I know this feels like a smack in the face because it is. But, you are so much more than you know, and if it takes me smacking you in the face with that fact, then it would have been worth it to awaken your champion.

It's hard to take the first steps to overcome any limiting beliefs that you may have. The rewards, however, will keep multiplying. Multiplying in every aspect of your life, your confidence will increase, and your outlook on the future and how you speak about it will change. As a result, the narrative of your entire life will change. Your life will change.

Irrespective of what your "one-day" dream may be. Be it opening your own business, finding happiness, traveling the world, a new home, etc.

Know this; many more people are saying "one day" than, today is the day I start taking steps to achieve my "one day."

Let's start by reframing our limiting beliefs, letting our champions do what they do best "win", and encouraging our friends and family to do the same. We need to do this within our communities to support, encourage and uplift each other. Because you are a 1-400trillion goddam special child, you overcame all the obstacles life threw at you to get to where you are today.

You are already winning and have the ability to do so much more. A shift in mindset will help you get there faster, achieve your "one day" sooner, and live your best life starting today.

If I could, you can!

It's up to you to take the next steps, it's up to you to put Mr. Shit where he belongs.

So make today the day that you decide enough is enough! Identify your limiting beliefs, reframe them, and realize that they are merely thoughts in your head that you can replace with positive thoughts at any time by doing the following.

Make some time each day for gratitude.

Always try and be of service whenever possible.

Actively support your goddamn fellow dreamers in reaching for their "one day." You are part of this tribe that will "one day" change the world

Keep a journal to help you stay focused and keep track of the amazing changes about to happen in your life.

The Dream Cast Project exists to be your partner in achieving your goals. So continue reading our "Believe in the Possible" series and get your hands on your own Becoming You Journal.

We hope our short read series "Believe in the possible" will inspire you to your "one day", not just for the next 24 hours, but for a lifetime, because you were born to be great and to share your gifts with the world.

Don't forget to follow us on TikTok, Instagram, Facebook and subscribe to our weekly inspirational newsletter.

It's time to boldly manifest the life you want

Write your own story and change the narrative of your life. Manifest your hopes and dreams and create your chosen reality. We create a journal for women and men that will help you do just that.

- It will help you to reflect on your identity and become who you are destined to be, strong and confident.

- It will help you heal from past emotional traumas. It will help you reduce stress and anxiety

- It will help you manage and understand your emotions.

- It will help you manifest your dreams, so they become your new reality.

- It will help you leave a legacy.

Could you or someone you care about benefit from a change in mindset? Could they use guidance on how to manifest their best future? Then this journal is for them.

This journal was designed specifically to help you create the life of your dreams.

It is a guided journal that is perfect for women and men of all ages and will guide them through prompts and activities to discover their greatness.

The Becoming You journal provides 12 powerful topics covering growth mindset, manifestation, abundance, and creating happiness for all women. Topics about how to change your mindset, change your narrative or change your life.

The Becoming You journal will help create a better world for yourself, those your care most about, and everyone around you.

Becoming You journal

For Women

Becoming You journal

For Men

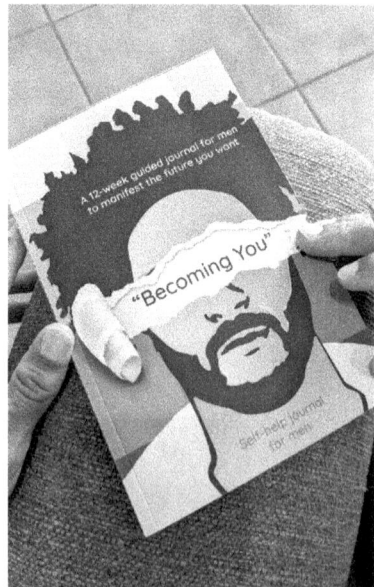

www.ingramcontent.com/pod-product-compliance
Lightning Source LLC
Chambersburg PA
CBHW060542030426

42337CB00021B/4387